This Walker book belongs to:

_____

_____

_____

For Dodo and all the others
D. K~S.

For Webs and Swifty
A. J.

*T*he author has based this book on the puppies
he and his family have known and loved over
a timespan of fifty years. When including the
author and his family in the pictures, the illus-
trator has chosen to show them at the same ages
throughout so as not to distract from the true
subject of the book – the puppies.

First published 1997 by Walker Books Ltd
87 Vauxhall Walk, London SE11 5HJ

This edition published 1999

4 6 8 10 9 7 5

Text © 1997 Foxbusters Ltd
Illustrations © 1997 Anita Jeram

The right of Dick King-Smith to be identified
as author of this work has been asserted by him
in accordance with the Copyright, Designs
and Patents Act 1988.

This book has been typeset in Monotype Horley Old Style.

Printed in China

British Library Cataloguing in Publication Data
A catalogue record for this book is
available from the British Library.

ISBN 978-0-7445-6348-1

www.walker.co.uk

PUPPY LOVE

written by
DICK KING-SMITH

illustrated by
ANITA JERAM

WALKER BOOKS
AND SUBSIDIARIES
LONDON · BOSTON · SYDNEY

I love baby animals of all sorts,
but especially I love puppies.

One of the reasons I love them so much is because they're so bumbling. It's the best word I can think of to describe a little animal that bounces about clumsily,

falling over its own feet and everyone else's,
tail wagging all the time, tongue ready to lick you,
and grinning all over its fat face!

Some people say that
puppies are naughty.
But when they do things
they shouldn't,

like chewing
holes in your slippers,

or upsetting tables
and breaking things,

or chasing
the cat,

or making a puddle
on the carpet,

it's not because
they are naughty.
It's just because
they are puppies.

We've had lots of puppies in our family –
from small ones like dachshunds and terriers,
to big ones like German Shepherds, and
even bigger ones like Great Danes.

Not to mention
mongrels of all
shapes and sizes.

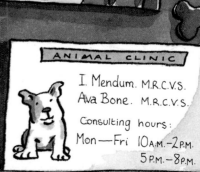

SAM

PRETTY POOCHES

1st

Best of Breed

ANIMAL CLINIC

I. Mendum. M.R.C.V.S.
Ava Bone. M.R.C.V.S.

Consulting hours:
Mon—Fri 10A.M.–2P.M.
5P.M.–8P.M.

One of the biggest puppies
we ever had was a Great Dane.

He was only
ten weeks old when
we brought him home,
but already he looked huge.

He lay down on the hearth-rug in front of
the fire and you could just see him thinking,
I may be very young but I'm already very
big, and from now on this hearth-rug
is my place to lie.

"What shall we call him?" we said to each other.
Something old-fashioned and gentlemanly,
we thought. We chose Humphrey.

Later on, when he was full grown,
Humphrey was always very careful
not to tread on any of the
little dogs that
we had.

And he was especially gentle with
puppies – even when they tried
to climb all over him,
or jumped up and
pulled at his tail.

One of the smallest puppies we ever had was a dachshund. We called her Dodo. I forget why. Maybe because it had been my grandfather's pet name for my grandmother.

I remember we drove a long way to collect her from the farm where the breeder lived.

Part of the farmhouse kitchen was taken up by a kind of huge dog-bed, covered in old rugs and blankets. And dachshunds – over fifteen of them, all adults except for one little puppy.

There she sat, perfectly happy,
amongst the grown-ups. She was the
last of her litter – her brothers and
sisters had all gone to new homes.
Now she would leave, too.

Her mother gave her
one last lick and a nuzzle,
and Dodo trotted towards us,
tail wagging,
ears flopping.

For us, it was
puppy love
at first sight.

Once home, we put her
down on the lawn and
introduced her to another
Great Dane we had then,
called Daniel. (It was long
after Humphrey's time.)

Most puppies would
have been terrified at the
sight of this monster.
Not Dodo.

Daniel lowered his great
head, while Dodo raised hers,
and they touched noses.

There are lots
of things puppies need
to learn when they first
come to live with you.
Like house-training.

We made sure we took Dodo
outside first thing in the morning,
last thing at night, after each meal,
and as often as we could in between.
Whenever she did anything
outside, we said, "Good girl!"
or "Good Dodo!".

There are lots of things puppies need you to do for them, too. When they're between eight and twelve weeks, you should take them to the vet's to be vaccinated. (Until then, be sure to keep them away from other dogs.)

They need a collar (with a disc
showing their name and address,
in case they get lost) and a lead.
By day, they need proper food
to eat and clean water to drink.
And at night, they should
have a bed of their own.

Most of all puppies need love.
There's nothing they like better
than to be stroked and scratched
and patted and played with.
They like lots of affection,
just like you do.

For some time now, we've only had one dog, called Little Elsie. She's Dodo's grand-daughter. But now she's got company. We've just bought a German Shepherd puppy, who's ten weeks old. We've called her Fly.

Fly is heavy and hairy,
and bumbling and bright and
beautiful. The garden looks
as if a tank has been through it.
It's full of her toys: my old slipper,
an ancient hearth-brush,
a rubber bone
that squeaks.

There are lots of things
Fly needs to learn,
and there are lots of things
Fly needs us to do for her.
But there's one thing she won't lack,
because she gets lots
of it already,
and that's …

puppy love!

Other books by Dick King-Smith and Anita Jeram

ISBN 978-1-4063-1196-9

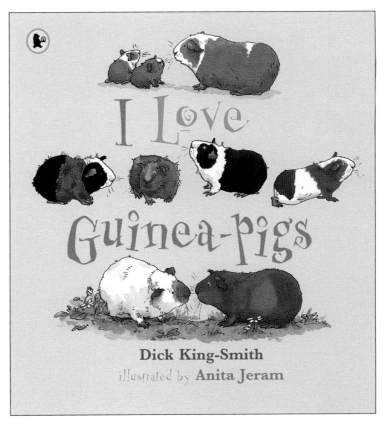

ISBN 978-1-4063-1872-2

Available from all good booksellers

www.walker.co.uk